KidCaps Presents

The Cuban Missile Crisis:
A History Just for Kids!

BOOKCAPS

KidCaps is An Imprint of BookCaps™
www.bookcaps.com

© 2013. All Rights Reserved.

Table of Contents

ABOUT KIDCAPS 3

INTRODUCTION 4

CHAPTER 1: WHAT LED UP TO THE CUBAN MISSILE CRISIS? 9

CHAPTER 2: WHY DID THE CUBAN MISSILE CRISIS HAPPEN? 15

CHAPTER 3: WHAT WAS IT LIKE TO BE A KID DURING THE CUBAN MISSILE CRISIS? 30

CHAPTER 4: HOW DID THE CUBAN MISSILE CRISIS END? 35

CHAPTER 5: WHAT HAPPENED AFTER THE CUBAN MISSILE CRISIS? 40

CONCLUSION 43

About KidCaps

KidCaps is an imprint of BookCaps™ that is just for kids! Each month BookCaps will be releasing several books in this exciting imprint. Visit are website or like us on Facebook to see more!

Introduction

Have you ever played a game of chess,. As you probably found out, chess is not too difficult to learn, but is difficult to master. Some people dedicate hours and hours to becoming the best chess player they can be, only to get beaten by someone else. But why is the game of chess so hard?

Chess, in case you have never played it, is like a miniature battle. Each player chooses a color (usually either white or black) and then take turns moving their pieces. But what makes chess so hard is that you have to try to capture the other player's king while trying to protect your own. Also, because you can only move one piece at a time, you have to try and think ahead and guess how the other player will react. Some of the best chess players are the ones who can understand what the other player is thinking and even predict what they will do with their pieces. They set traps, have surprise attacks, and plan their moves carefully.

The game of chess has been used by some people to describe war. Like two players who have to decide what piece to move where and how to react to what the other player does, during a war government leaders have to decide how to use their militaries against their enemies and which battles to fight and which ones to avoid. They have to react quickly and try to think ahead. Some of the most successful wars ever fought were the ones where the leaders learned to think like their enemies and to predict their actions.

After the second World War, two powerful nations found themselves fighting against each other, and for some people it looked like a big game of chess. Each side had to think carefully about what decisions to make and about how the other side would react to it. These two nations were the United States of America and the Union of Soviet Socialist Republics (the USSR), and the fight was called the Cold War. This struggle between the two powerful countries was called a Cold War because there was no direct fighting between the militaries on each side. Instead, the fighting had more to do with words and laws passed, spies trying to get information, and sometimes with helping other countries to fight each other, where each one represented a side in the Cold War. How long did things go on like that? The Cold War lasted for about 44 years, and on a few occasions the Cold War heated up quite a bit and almost became a real war, one that would have led to World War Three.

In this book, we will be talking about one of those occasions: the Cuban Missile Crisis. Have you ever heard of the Cuban Missile Crisis or what happened then? As we saw earlier, the key to being a good chess player is to try and understand what the other player is thinking and what they want. The same is true of being a good president or military leader. The Cuban Missile Crisis was a serious moment during the Cold War when many people thought that a nuclear war was about to begin, which would have meant the deaths of millions of people. How was such a complete disaster avoided during the Cuban Missile Crisis? The Secretary of Defense of the United States at the time, Robert McNamara, later said during an interview: "In the Cuban Missile Crisis, at the end, I think we did put ourselves in the skin of the Soviets."[1]

So as you read this book, try to do the same thing that the leaders back then did: try to understand what both sides were thinking and what both sides wanted to happen during the crisis. Although some pretty scary things happened during the Cuban Missile Crisis, when you stop to think about them you can often see that there were some logical reasons behind the decisions that each side made. So in this book we won't actually be talking about "good guys" and "bad guys"; we will be talking about two large nations that didn't trust each other and how they tried to prevent a nuclear war from happening. We will also see how the whole situation got more complicated when a third military leader, named Fidel Castro, got angry with both the USA and the USSR.

So what can you expect to learn in this book? The first section will talk about what led up to the Cuban Missile Crisis. We will learn a little bit more about the Cold War and people involved. We will also see how Cuba became a Communist country and a friend of the USSR. Did you know that the United States had taken aggressive steps against Fidel Castro to

---

[1] Quotation source: http://www.errolmorris.com/film/fow_transcript.html

take him out of power? All of those conditions helped to set the stage for the Cuban Missile Crisis.

The next section will help us to see why the Cuban Missile Crisis happened. Although no one wanted to start a nuclear war, it almost happened. Why did the USSR put nuclear weapons on the small island of Cuba, and why did Fidel Castro allow it? Why did the United States get so scared when they saw the weapons? We will also see how this situation created some truly unique challenges for everyone involved.

The next section will dive into what happened during the crisis. We will get to sit with President John F. Kennedy and the Executive Committee of the National Security Council (EXCOMM) as they consider their options and try to imagine how the USSR's Premier (leader) Nikita Khrushchev will react to them. We will see how the United States finally chose to act, and how close the world came to having a nuclear war, especially on a day during the crisis called "Black Saturday". We will also see some of the personal struggles that President Kennedy had to deal with as he tried to figure out what to do.

The next section will show us what it was like to be a kid back then. A kid living during the Cold War and the Cuban Missile Crisis would have seen how quickly things can change. Almost overnight, everyone went from thinking that tomorrow would be just another day to thinking that a nuclear war was about to break out. We will see how families everywhere were affected by the news of the Cuban

Missile Crisis, especially after President Kennedy talked about it in a special news report.

The section after that will help us to see <u>how the Cuban Missile Crisis ended</u>. The solution was decided by just a few people living thousands of miles apart from each other, and in the end there were no nuclear bombs dropped on anybody.

But the following section will show us <u>what happened after the crisis ended</u>, and how there was a second, smaller, and more secretive Cuban Missile Crisis, one that only recently was talked about in the world's newspapers. We will learn how even after the USA and USSR agreed to remove the big nuclear missiles that Cuba's President Fidel Castro still had some plans to do something dangerous against the American people, and the only person who knew about it was the Soviet Ambassador. How did this second crisis come to an end, and what steps did the USA and USSR take to prevent a nuclear war from ever happening? We will find out in this section.

The Cuban Missile Crisis only lasted for 13 days, but it taught everyone involved a lot of lessons. Even though the USSR no longer exists, there are still lots of nuclear bombs in the world today, and there are still lots of ways for a big war to start. The lessons learned about learning to think like the enemy thinks and trying to predict what they will do are still important things that every president tries to do. As you read this book, try to see if you can learn any other lessons from the Cuban Missile Crisis.

Are you ready to learn more? Then let's get started!

Chapter 1: What led up to the Cuban Missile Crisis?

World War Two was fought primarily in Europe, trying to stop the aggression of Germany against its European neighbors. One of the nations that Germany attacked was Communist Russia. The Russians were able to defend their country against the Germans and eventually pushed the Germans back all the way to their capital city of Berlin in 1945. After the war, Russia made some notable agreements (called "treaties") with many countries in Eastern Europe and the USSR became the leader of a Communist superpower.

In the meantime, the other nations decided to make special alliances and treaties of their own, and the most powerful country after the war, the United States, took the lead as a second superpower. The two countries used laws and political speeches to try to convince the world that they were right and that the other side was wrong. And from time to time, the USSR would support one country in a fight while the USA would support another, and they would fight something called a "proxy war", a war that is fought using other nations' soldiers, and not your own.

The United States thought that if more countries became Communist then the USSR would get stronger and eventually force everyone to do things their way. So, they tried to stop other countries from becoming Communist, including Korea in 1950 and later on Vietnam in 1965. It became a kind of normal thing to use other countries to fight against each other. But for a long time the fighting seemed isolated from the United States, in far off places like Asia. But in 1959, all of that changed.

For some years, the situation in Cuba had not been easy for many of its citizens. While there was a high standard of living for some Cubans, others were extremely poor and felt like the government didn't care about them. The leaders that they had chosen seemed to make the situation even worse so many Cubans decided that they wanted a change. In 1959, a Communist movement led by Fidel Castro was able to chase the Cuban President out of the country and to take over the country. Lots of lands and businesses came under the control of the new Communist government, and the people hoped that their future would be better in the hands of Fidel Castro.

In the meantime, the United States became worried about this new government. We already know how the USA felt about Communism, so imagine how nervous some people in Washington DC felt about having a Communist country just 90 miles away their borders! In the meantime, Cuba started a close friendship with the USSR, who started to send ships full of food and weapons to Cuba.

Can you see how things started to get dangerous? It's like building a house with playing cards: each time you add a new card the house gets more unstable and closer to falling down. Each time the USSR did something to make Cuba stronger, and each time that the USA did something to make Cuba weaker, the house of cards got taller and more fragile, and if it fell down it would mean war between the world's two superpowers.

So now we have the situation where the USSR is trying to help Cuba, but the USA doesn't want that to happen. In the meantime, both the USA and the USSR are trying to build as many weapons as they can just in case there is a war. They think that by building so many weapons maybe they can scare the other side into never attacking them. Many of the weapons built during this time period (called the "arms race") are nuclear bombs that are attached to rockets which can be launched over long distances, anywhere from 1,000 to 3,000 miles away. Some of these missiles were portable and were put onto military bases around the world. For example, the United States installed some nuclear missiles on a military base in Turkey, just to the south of the USSR.

Because the United States didn't trust either the USSR or Cuba, they decided to start flying unique spy planes, called U2 planes, over Cuba to take pictures of what was going on there.

A U2 spy place could take pictures of people on the ground from high up in the sky[2]

While on a routine mission to take secret pictures of Cuba and of what was going on there, a U2 spy plane flying over Cuba on October 14, 1962, took the following picture:

---

[2] Image source: http://www.npr.org/blogs/alltechconsidered/2012/05/28/153582693/vintage-spy-plane-gives-high-tech-drone-a-run-for-its-money

Can you see the missiles in the above picture?[3]

The picture clearly showed what were called "medium range" missiles being assembled in Cuba. The missiles were compared to photos, and it was discovered that they had come from the USSR.

Now nuclear missiles capable of being fired at targets almost 1,000 miles away were parked in the United States' backyard, just 90 miles off of the coast of Florida, and they were under the control of a Communist government that did not like Americans! How would President Kennedy respond? Would the USSR encourage the Cubans to use the weapons? How could nuclear war be avoided?

The Cuban Missile Crisis had begun.

---

[3] Image source: http://blogs.cfr.org/lindsay/2012/10/16/twe-remembers-learning-more-about-the-cuban-missile-crisis/

Chapter 2: Why Did the Cuban Missile Crisis Happen?

Do you remember what makes chess such a difficult game to play? Both players have to be thinking about how to capture the enemy's king while still protecting their own. In other words, they have to play *offensive* (attack) and *defensive* (protection) at the same time. When the USSR put about 40 nuclear missiles on Cuba in 1962, it was a chess move that made both sides stop and think about what they were going to do next. How could they protect themselves but still try and hurt the other guy?

Like the US Secretary of Defense, Robert McNamara, said in the introduction, the United States tried to put itself "in the skin" of the Soviets, to try and think like they did. Both sides tried to understand what the other person was thinking and how they would react to the situation. Let's look a little bit at what was motivating each country's actions during the Cuban Missile Crisis: we will try and get into the skin of the USSR, of Cuba, and of the USA.

The USSR lay across the Atlantic Ocean from the United States on one side and across the Bering Strait (near Alaska) on the other. But even so, it felt like the

United States had soldiers everywhere in Europe and military bases in all of the countries near the USSR. In fact, the United States had even placed large missiles with nuclear bombs in Turkey, which put them extremely close to USSR cities and citizens. The Soviets felt like they could be attacked at any moment by the United States and that they would not have a chance to defend themselves. So, they thought: "What if we do the same thing? What if we put some of our nuclear missiles in a friendly country that is near the United States? That way, in case we are attacked by the United States we can defend ourselves more quickly. In fact, the United States will probably decide not to ever attack us if they know that we have bombs in Cuba."

Can you understand the point of view of the USSR? Can you see why they thought that it was a good chess move to put their missiles on the small island of Cuba? They thought that it would be a good way to protect themselves and to make sure that the USA never used nuclear bombs against them. Premier Nikita Khrushchev thought that he had found a terrific way to balance the power a little more during the Cold War.

But what about Cuba? Why did Fidel Castro allow the USSR to place nuclear missiles on his island, knowing that doing so might lead to a war with the much larger and more powerful United States? Although he had only been in power for about three years by this time, Fidel Castro had already been the target of many attacks organized by the United States.

In an interview, Secretary of Defense Robert McNamara said:

> "But, more importantly, from a Cuban and a Russian point of view, they knew what in a sense I really didn't know: we had attempted to assassinate Castro under Eisenhower and under Kennedy and later under Johnson. And in addition to that, major voices in the U.S. were calling for invasion."[4]

Did you understand what the United States had been doing in Cuba just before the crisis? They had been trying to *kill* President Fidel Castro. In fact, On April 17, 1961, the United States had even tried to organize an invasion of Cuba using Cuban exiles (Cubans who had been kicked out of their country). The operation was called the Bay of Pigs Invasion, and it was not successful. President Castro himself took the lead in fighting back against the invaders, and he became more convinced than ever that the United States would never be his friend and that they wanted him dead.

---

[4] Quotation source: http://www.errolmorris.com/film/fow_transcript.html

A picture of the Bay of Pigs invasion[5]

President Castro began to receive weapons from the USSR that he could use to defend himself. But during a secret meeting between him and Premier Khrushchev in July of 1962, it was decided to send the nuclear missiles that the USSR and Cuba could use for protection and as part of a "first strike" (or first attack) plan. Fidel Castro felt that his small and new government would finally have some permanent protection and security.

Now what about the United States? What were President Kennedy and the rest of his government thinking about the missiles being put onto Cuba? The President saw this chess move as a direct threat to the

[5] Image source: http://wlcentral.org/node/1662

safety of the American people. He and his advisors thought that the Soviets would use the missiles to start a nuclear war. In fact, they were kind of right. The Soviets who went to Cuba to help set up the missiles had permission to launch them according to their own judgment, so, in theory, they may have chosen to launch the missiles if they felt threatened enough.

The pictures taken by the spy planes showed that the missiles wouldn't be ready for about two weeks, so the United States had to decide how to act. They felt that they were threatened and that the actions of the USSR and Cuba were too aggressive and not simply a question of defense.

The USSR, Cuba, and the USA all were involved in this situation. The three leaders would have to make some tough decisions, and millions of lives would be affected by those decisions. As each of the governments tried to predict how the other was going to react, the soldiers on the ground in Cuba kept working to get the missiles ready to fire. The clock was ticking.

What happened during the Cuban Missile Crisis?

President Kennedy meets with his advisors to resolve the Cuban Missile Crisis[6]

Both the United States and the USSR, the two main players in the Cuban Missile Crisis, had to figure out how to get what they wanted without losing it all. Neither of them wanted a full on war, but neither of them wanted to back down either and make the other one look like the winner. How could they ever figure it out?

The first step for President Kennedy was to look for help. He decided to form a special group of people who could decide what the best solution would be. Called the Executive Committee of the National Security Council (EXCOMM), this group had to decide how best to handle the Soviet's actions. It was

---

[6] Image source: http://www.jfklibrary.org/Asset-Viewer/ZgLsd8Qx0kefPPeR3VK-7w.aspx

clear that the President could not just sit back and do nothing, so another course of action had to be chosen. What were the options first considered by the President?

1) Bomb the missile locations only
2) Bomb larger targets to weaken Cuba
3) Bomb larger targets to weaken Cuba and then invade Cuba with American soldiers

No one actually liked those options because they meant a direct conflict with a close friend of the USSR. As part of their chess game, the Americans tried to predict what the USSR would do if they bombed and invaded Cuba. EXCOMM came to the conclusion that Premier Khrushchev would do the same thing to the Americans. If the Americans attacked a friend of the USSR, then the USSR would attack a friend of the Americans, probably a target somewhere in Europe.

Like all good chess players, the Americans and the Soviets tried to think two, three, and even four moves into the future. They knew that if the Soviets attacked an American target (like Berlin, for example), then the Americans would be forced to keep their treaty agreements and to defend that target, which would then want to fight against the USSR. Within a short time, many countries could become involved in the conflict, and it was possible that nuclear weapons would be used in war, just as the Americans had used them during World War Two in Japan.

President Kennedy and his EXCOMM were not interested in starting World War Three, but what other option could there be? Adlai Stevenson II, who was acting as the United States' Ambassador to the United Nations, suggested making some sort of a deal with the Soviets in order to keep the peace. He suggested removing the American nuclear missiles from Turkey in exchange for the Soviets' removing theirs from Cuba. But that idea was not popular with anyone in the room, especially not with President Kennedy. Do you know why?

When you give an aggressor (someone who starts a fight) what they want, politicians have a special word for it: *appeasement*. During World War Two, President Kennedy's father, Joseph P. Kennedy, had been the United States' Ambassador to Great Britain. When the Germans invaded different countries in Europe and eventually sent bombs over the English Channel to London, Joseph Kennedy recommended giving the Germans what they wanted and hoping that the fighting would stop. Of course, it was later shown to be a terrible idea that only encouraged German leader Adolf Hitler, and Ambassador Kennedy was quickly encouraged to resign from his job.

President John F. Kennedy did not like the idea of bombing Cuba in a sort of sneak attack and looking like big bullies. But at the same time, the United States felt that they could not simply sit back and let the USSR put these missiles in Cuba. President Kennedy explained his thinking while trying to find a solution:

> [If] we do nothing, they have a missile base there with all the pressure that brings to bear on the United States and damage to our prestige. If we attack Cuban missiles or Cuba … we would be regarded as the trigger-happy Americans who lost Berlin. We would have no support among our allies. Which leaves me only one alternative, which is to fire nuclear weapons – which is a hell of an alternative – and begin a nuclear exchange, with all this happening."[7]

President Kennedy did not want people to think that he was trying to do anything to avoid war, as his father had been accused of doing. But he didn't want to be accused of being a big bully either. Was there a third solution, something better than doing nothing but not so serious as bombing and invading Cuba? After long days and hours of talks, EXCOMM came up with a workable plan: "quarantine".

What is "quarantine"? Quarantine is the same thing as a blockade, which is where a lot of ships surround the main ports of a country to prevent certain types of things from getting into or moving out of the country. But President Kennedy did not want to call the action a "blockade", because that is actually an act of war, something that everyone was trying to avoid. EXCOMM decided to give the Soviets an official

---

[7] Quotation source: http://www.dailymail.co.uk/news/article-2207946/Revealed-JFKs-stabbing-generals-mocked-President-battled-avoid-regarded-trigger-happy-Americans-lost-Berlin.html

demand to remove the missiles from the island of Cuba and to respect the quarantine. He announced the plans to the American people on October 22, 1962, during a special televised speech.

President Kennedy tells the American people about the situation in Cuba[8]

In his speech, President Kennedy tried to explain to his fellow citizens why the missiles were so dangerous, and why he felt that action had to be taken. Here are some highlights from his October 22 speech:

> "Nuclear weapons are so destructive and ballistic missiles are so swift, that any substantially increased possibility of their use

[8] Image source: http://www.britannica.com/EBchecked/media/74998/President-John-F-Kennedy-announcing-the-US-naval-blockade-of

or any sudden change in their deployment may well be regarded as a definite threat to peace. For many years, both the Soviet Union and the United States, recognizing this fact, have deployed strategic nuclear weapons with great care, never upsetting the precarious status quo which insured that these weapons would not be used in the absence of some vital challenge...The 1930's taught us a clear lesson: aggressive conduct, if allowed to go unchecked and unchallenged, ultimately leads to war.

I have directed that the following initial steps be taken immediately:

First: To halt this offensive buildup a strict quarantine on all offensive military equipment under shipment to Cuba is being initiated. All ships of any kind bound for Cuba from whatever nation or port will, if found to contain cargoes of offensive weapons, be turned back. This quarantine will be extended, if needed, to other types of cargo and carriers. We are not at this time, however, denying the necessities of life as the Soviets attempted to do in their Berlin blockade of 1948.

Finally: I call upon Chairman Khrushchev to halt and eliminate this clandestine, reckless, and provocative threat to world peace and to stable relations between our two nations."[9]

---

[9] Quotation source:

In this speech, can you hear how serious President Kennedy's tone of voice must have been? What do you think it might have felt like to listen to those words live, in your living room, with your family? Would you have been afraid? Many American people were sure that a war was about to start and that it was going to be a catastrophic war.

The quarantine began to be enforced almost right away, and many Soviet ships stopped just short of the agreed spot on the ocean. Others tried to push through, but it was discovered that they were just carrying food and so they were allowed to pass. Two aircraft carriers, several destroyers, cruisers, and planes from air bases in Florida all patrolled the waters and made sure that nothing got into or left Cuba unless the USA said so.

http://www.americanrhetoric.com/speeches/jfkcubanmissilecrisis.html

Planes and ships enforced the quarantine[10]

The quarantine worked well, but after a few days it seemed that nothing much was changing. Spy plane pictures showed that the Soviets were still trying to get the missiles assembled and ready to use, and there was no sign that they had any plans of removing them from the island. For a lot of people, it looked like this chess game had reached a stalemate: that's the word used to describe the situation where nobody wins and everybody loses.

---

[10] Image source: http://www.historycentral.com/Sixties/Cuban.html

28

On Saturday, October 27, after the quarantine had been in effect for several days, a series of events happened all at once that made the whole world think that war was about to happen. Some of those involved would later call October 27 "Black Saturday". Why? On that day, two U2 planes disappeared; one was shot down by the Soviets while flying over Cuba and the other disappeared while flying over Asia. Soviet troops completed preparation of the nuclear warheads and the nearby American military base Guantanamo Bay was targeted by them as part of an invasion.

Submarines, which had been in the water outside of Cuba, were being followed by American ships, who dropped small explosive into the water to signal them to come to the surface. One of the Soviet submarines, the *B-59*, had been underwater for several days and out of radio contact with their superiors. Some of the men thought that the small explosions overhead might be attacks from the Americans and that a war had begun since they lost radio contact with Moscow (the capital of the USSR). The captain of the *B*-59 was ready to fire the nuclear torpedoes, but second-in-command Officer Vasili Arkhipov wanted to wait and helped to calm the captain down. If the captain would have fired the torpedo, you can imagine what the results would have been. Thomas Blanton, director of the national Security archive, later said: "The lesson from this is that a guy called Vasili Arkhipov saved the world."[11]

---

[11] Quotation source: http://www.latinamericanstudies.org/cold-war/sovietsbomb.htm

Some of the key people involved thought that the world wasn't going to survive to see another Saturday. Plans were made to evacuate the President in case a nuclear bomb was fired at Washington DC, and some of the members of the government told their families to be ready to leave the city at a moment's notice. It was the most tense day of the Cuban Missile Crisis, and it looked like things weren't going to be getting better any time soon.

Chapter 3: What Was it Like to Be a Kid During the Cuban Missile Crisis?

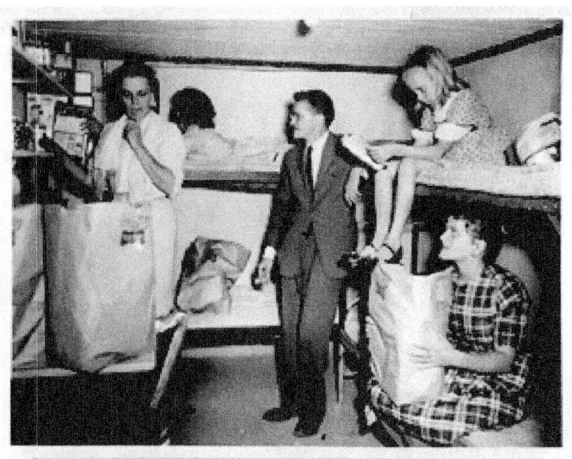

A family in their bomb shelter; Kids practice hiding from a nuclear bomb explosion[12]

Can you imagine what it would have been like to be a kid during the Cuban Missile Crisis? Unlike other wars that we fought far away and never truly affected

---

[12] Image sources: http://writemesomethingbeautiful.com/1/fallout-shelter-my-ass/; http://apps.detnews.com/apps/history/index.php?id=48

anyone back home, the Cuban Missile Crisis felt like it was in America's backyard. People across the country began to think seriously about what life would be like if a nuclear war broke out between the USSR and the USA. Even before the Cuban Missile Crisis, Americans knew how dangerous nuclear bombs could be. Look at the magazine below, published in early 1962:

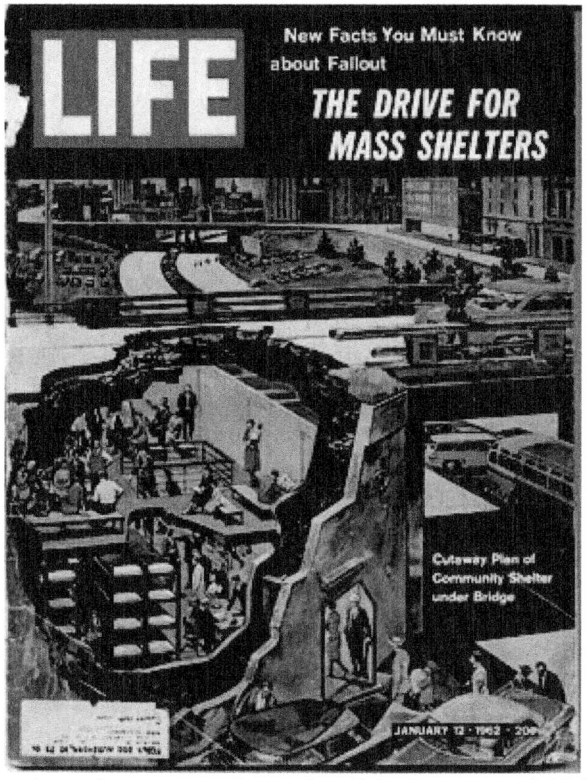

An American magazine printed in January of 1962 talked about emergency shelters[13]

---

[13] Image source: http://writemesomethingbeautiful.com/1/fallout-

People were already thinking about how to build a structure that could stand up not only against the huge explosion from a nuclear bomb but also against the poison air and dust that it created. Once the missiles arrived in Cuba and the quarantine started, many Americans rushed to the stored to buy lots of canned food to put in their bomb shelters, just in case. Can you imagine going to the store with your mom or dad, seeing the long lines, the full shopping carts, and the empty shelves. Would you have been scared about what was going on?

Then, at least once or twice a year in most schools, the kids had to practice what they would do just in case a nuclear bomb exploded in their town. As you can see in the picture at the beginning of this section, the kids would have to hide under their desks and curl up into little balls, protected from the flying glass of the windows. The looks on the faces of the kids make it pretty clear that they didn't like having to think about so scary like a nuclear missile landing near their school.

Kids could tell when the adults were scared, and imagine how some of them must of felt when their fathers and mothers made plans for them to leave the big city, "just in case". What would you have done? A lot of kids would worry about the friends that they left behind and about their house and their school. But in a time of emergency, some parents felt that running

---

shelter-my-ass/

away from the big cities like Washington DC and New York was the safest thing to do.

As you watched the news and heard President Kennedy talking, so you think that you would understood everything that he said and why he was so upset about the missiles in Cuba? Would you have agreed that something needed to be done, even if it led to war? Or would have thought that maybe the missiles could be left there, just like the US missiles would be left in Turkey? Or maybe you would have agreed with Ambassador Stevenson who suggested a trade, although some people thought that it looked like appeasement.

Being a kid back then would have been tough. After all, sometimes adults don't give kids all the facts maybe because they think that kids may not understand it or because they may not be able to handle the truth. But if your parents had sat you down and explained everything, would you have agreed with President Kennedy's choice to establish the quarantine or not? It's easy to look back at a chess game and know which moves were good ones and which ones were mistakes, but in the middle of the game it's not always so easy to be sure of the decisions that the players are making.

Chapter 4: How Did the Cuban Missile Crisis End?

October 27, known as Black Saturday, was the day when the world seemed closest to war. With one plane being shot down by the Soviets, another disappearing over Asia, and a crisis on a submarine with nuclear torpedoes onboard, it looked like everyone who had prepared for the worst was right. But then the President decided to respond to a message that he had received the day before, on October 26. The message was written by Premier Khrushchev himself, and it looked like there might be an opportunity for peace. In his emotional letter, Khrushchev suggested that if the United States promised not to invade Cuba, the missile would no longer be necessary and would be quietly removed. Note some other highlights from the long message:

> "If assurances were given by the President and the Government of the United States that the USA itself would not participate in an attack on Cuba and would restrain others from actions of this sort, if you would recall your fleet, this would immediately change everything. I am not speaking for Fidel Castro, but I think that he and the Government

of Cuba, evidently, would declare demobilization and would appeal to the people to get down to peaceful labor. Then, too, the question of armaments would disappear, since, if there is no threat, then armaments are a burden for every people.

If, however, you have not lost your self-control and sensibly conceive what this might lead to, then, Mr. President, we and you ought not now to pull on the ends of the rope in which you have tied the knot of war because the more the two of us pull, the tighter that knot will be tied. And a moment may come when that knot will be tied so tight that even he who tied it will not have the strength to untie it, and then it will be necessary to cut that knot, and what that would mean is not for me to explain to you, because you yourself understand perfectly of what terrible forces our countries dispose."[14]

Premier Khrushchev was scared, just like President Kennedy and everyone else involved. Nobody wanted this war to happen, but it seemed like events were getting out of control and that the men who were supposed to be in charge weren't truly in control anymore. This message was written by the hand of Khrushchev himself, and it wasn't clear whether or not his fellow politicians approved the message. But it was clear that the message left the door open for a

---

[14] Quotation source: http://microsites.jfklibrary.org/cmc/oct26/doc4.html

peaceful end to the crisis. But then, on October 27, a second message arrived from the USSR, and it was clear that Khrushchev was not behind this one.

The tone of the letter was utterly different. Instead of one leader speaking to another and trying to make sure that no one went to war, this letter was much more direct and tried to bargain with the United States in order to resolve the crisis and to protect the reputation of the USSR. Here is part of the second message received:

> "You are disturbed over Cuba. You say that this disturbs you because it is ninety miles by sea from the coast of the United States of America. But...you have placed destructive missile weapons, which you call offensive, in Turkey, literally next to us [there is not even 90 miles of distance]...I therefore make this proposal: We are willing to remove from Cuba the means which you regard as offensive...[if you] will remove its analogous means from Turkey...And after that, persons entrusted by the United Nations Security Council could inspect on the spot the fulfillment of the pledges made."[15]

Can you see how the second message has a totally different personality to it? Instead of one man trying to make peace and explain his reasoning to another

---

[15] Quotation source: http://www.marxists.org/history/cuba/subject/missile-crisis/ch03.htm

man, this message accused the United States of having caused the problem in the first place and then went on to set strict conditions about how to resolve the crisis. Did you see what the USSR wanted President Kennedy to do? They wanted the USA to remove their nuclear weapons from Turkey, and to make an announcement to the public that they were going to do so. How do you think President Kennedy reacted to the second message?

As we saw before, President Kennedy did not feel like he could publically announce the removal of the missiles in Turkey (even though the missiles were older models and not too useful anymore). Why not? Because it would look like the United States was appeasing the USSR and giving in to their demands. The USA felt like a parent whose child had been kidnapped for ransom. They were worried that if they paid the ransom to get the kid back then the kidnapper would just turn around and do the same thing all over again with a different child. They thought that the USSR might try to put more missiles in a different country and then demand something else. So how would President Kennedy and the US government react? The world was watching.

The White House came up with an interesting solution: answer the first letter and ignore the second letter. In other words, publically declare that the United States had no plans of invading Cuba and then make plans for the USSR to remove the missiles. But in order to make sure that the Soviets would cooperate, the White House sent a secret message through a few trusted people that if the Cuban missiles were removed, then within a short time the missiles in Turkey would be quietly taken out of the country.

It didn't take long for the Soviets to respond. The next day, Sunday October 28, the Soviets agreed to the terms and started making plans to remove the missiles. By the end of November, Americans were happy to see Soviet boats carrying missiles headed away from Cuba and back towards the USSR.

The crisis had been resolved, and no nuclear missiles had been fired. Although there was no clear loser, it looked like everybody had won: they had avoided starting World War Three.

Chapter 5: What Happened After the Cuban Missile Crisis?

Cuban President Fidel Castro with Soviet Ambassador to the USA Anatoly Dobrynin [16]

It looked like a nuclear war, and world disaster was avoided when the Soviets decided to remove their nuclear missiles from Cuba on October 28. But there was still one little problem left, something that even the United States did not know about: there were still more nuclear weapons on Cuba that had been kept a secret.

[16] Image source: http://www.guardian.co.uk/commentisfree/2012/oct/22/cuban-missile-crisis-nikita-khrushchev

Along with the 40 or so mid- and long-range nuclear missiles that the U2 plane took pictures of, there were also over 100 tactical nuclear weapons. What is a tactical nuclear weapon? Instead of being a large bomb that can be sent from one country to another using a rocket, tactical nuclear weapons are small enough to be fired by tanks and artillery guns. While the explosions may be smaller, they are still dangerous weapons; and Cuba had 100 of them.

Fidel Castro was not happy about how the crisis had been handled. He felt that he had not been included in the secret negotiation and felt that the USSR had simply used him and his country like a piece on the chessboard. He also felt that the Americans were now exercising control over him by saying what weapons his country could and could not have. Now that the Soviet missiles were leaving, he felt more vulnerable and unprotected than ever.

After it was announced that the Soviets would be removing the large nuclear weapons, President Castro practically begged the Soviet Ambassador, Anatoly Dobrynin, to leave the smaller weapons in Cuba. But Ambassador Dobrynin knew that the United States would be upset if Cuba had them and that Fidel Castro was unpredictable. It was possible that Castro would use them against the Americans and end up starting World War Three, the very thing that the USSR and USA had worked so hard to avoid. What could Ambassador Dobrynin do? The choice was simple: he lied.

Ambassador Dobrynin lied to Fidel Castro and told him that the Soviets had laws against leaving the tactical nuclear weapons with a foreign country. After all, all of the Soviet soldiers were going home, and they must take all Soviet property with them. Although he didn't like the answer, President Castro accepted it.

By the end of April, 1962 (six months after the crisis ended) the US missiles in Turkey had been disassembled and removed. The USA and USSR took steps to make sure that open lines of communication could exist between the two governments from that moment forward. A special direct line of communication (called "The Hotline") was installed in capital building of each country so as to avoid any misunderstandings that could lead to nuclear war in the future.

The USSR and the USA still didn't trust each other enough to stop their arms race, and both sides kept trying to build as many nuclear missiles as they could. However, instead of focusing on medium- and long-range weapons, both sides (especially the USSR) began to focus mostly on ICBMs (Inter-Continental Ballistic Missiles), which were bombs that could be launched from home and hit targets anywhere in the world.

The Cuban Missile crisis had ended, but the Cold War was a long way from ending.

Conclusion

We have learned a lot about this important time in history. Were you able to try and look at the whole thing as if it were a chess game, and to see how each side tried to predict what the other one would do? It was also interesting to see how both the USSR and the USA tried to get what they wanted from the other side while still protecting themselves. The world came to the brink of nuclear war, but at the last minute secret negotiations were able to resolve the crisis.

Do you remember everything that we learned today? Let's have a quick review.

The first section talked about <u>what led up to the Cuban Missile Crisis</u>. We learned a little bit more about the Cold War and people involved. We also saw how Cuba became a Communist country and a friend of the USSR. Basically, because they had similar political ideas and goals, the USSR wanted to help Cuba to become stronger and more stable after its revolution. But did you see how the United States took aggressive steps against Fidel Castro to take him out of power? According to the Secretary of defense Robert McNamara, the USA had tried to assassinate Fidel Castro. All of those conditions helped to set the stage for the Cuban Missile Crisis.

The next section helped us to see why the Cuban Missile Crisis happened. Although no one wanted to start a nuclear war, it almost happened. Why did the USSR put nuclear weapons on the small island of Cuba, and why did Fidel Castro allow it? As you may remember, both countries were actually trying to defend themselves against an attack by the United States! The USSR felt threatened by American nuclear missiles in nearby Turkey, and Cuba felt threatened after repeated assassination attempts and a failed invasion. But why did the United States get so scared when they saw the weapons? They saw the missiles as a first-strike weapon, meant to start a nuclear war. We also saw how this situation created some unique challenges for everyone involved.

The next section dove into what happened during the crisis. We got to sit with President John F. Kennedy and the Executive Committee of the National Security Council (EXCOMM) as they considered their options and tried to imagine how the USSR's Premier (leader) Nikita Khrushchev would react to them. We saw how the United States finally chose to act (establishing a quarantine) and how close the world came to having a nuclear war. We saw how one day during the crisis, a day called "Black Saturday", things almost got seriously bad. A plane was shot down, a submarine almost used their nuclear torpedoes, and an aggressive message was sent by the USSR to the USA. In that section, we also saw some of the personal struggles that President Kennedy had to deal with as he tried to figure out what to do. He wanted to make it clear to everyone that he was not like his father and that he would not consider appeasement as a real option to solve the crisis.

The section after that one showed us <u>what it was like to be a kid back then</u>. A kid living during the Cold War and the Cuban Missile Crisis would have seen how quickly things can change. Almost overnight, everyone went from thinking that tomorrow would be just another day to thinking that a nuclear war was about to break out. We will see how families everywhere were affected by the news of the Cuban Missile Crisis, especially after President Kennedy talked about it in a special news report. Some people went crazy buying all sorts of canned foods, while others built special bomb shelters in their homes just in case.

The section after that helped us to see <u>how the Cuban Missile Crisis ended</u>. The solution was decided by just a few people living thousands of miles apart from each other, and in the end there were no nuclear bombs dropped on anybody. The secret communications between the two sides helped to resolve the crisis. The USA promised not to attack Cuba and secretly agreed to remove their missiles from Turkey. And the USSR agreed to remove the missiles from Cuba.

Finally, the last section showed us <u>what happened after the crisis ended</u>, and how there was a second, smaller, and more secretive Cuban Missile Crisis, one that only recently was talked about in the world's newspapers. We will learn how even after the USA and USSR agreed to remove the big nuclear missiles that Cuba's President Fidel Castro still had some plans to do something dangerous against the American people, and the only person who knew about it was the Soviet Ambassador. Do you remember how this second crisis came to an end? The Soviet ambassador lied to President Castro and told him that it was against the law for the Soviets to leave any of their weapons with a foreign government. Can you imagine some of the bad things that may have happened if the USSR had left those tactical nuclear weapons in Fidel Castro's hands? We also saw the steps that the USA and USSR took to prevent a nuclear war from ever happening, which included installing a direct communications system called "The Hotline".

The Cuban Missile Crisis was the closest the world ever got to a real nuclear exchange, with two or more countries launching these deadly weapons at each other. While the Cold War may now be over, do you think something like the Cuban Missile Crisis could ever happen again? If so, let's hope that the leaders involved try to be smart and not be too quick to use nuclear weapons. Otherwise, the world may see a war from which it will never recover.

Printed in Great Britain
by Amazon